AN INTRODUCT

ETHICS

MORALITY

AND

VIRTUES

FOR CHILDREN

TONY FRAIS

Copyright © Tony Frais 2018

Published in 2018 by Frais Publishing
Leeds
United Kingdom

Email afrais@tiscali.co.uk

ISBN 978-0-9548068-5-9

CONTENTS

TEACHER'S INTRODUCTION TO THE COURSE

The teaching of ethics, morality and virtues in schools is becoming increasingly recognised as important by education experts. Research has also shown that 84% of UK parents believe that teachers should encourage good morals and values in their students.

This short introduction course is designed to make pupils aware of and learn about the key concepts of ethics, morality and virtues which are considered as important for character development. The pupils will have the opportunity to discuss the points raised by each subject of the virtues by answering and discussing the questions asked.

The course is recommended to be taught to ages 10-11.

The course has been designed so that it does not require any specialist teacher training, or extensive lesson planning.

THE MEANING OF ETHICS, MORALITY AND VIRTUES

At its simplest, ethics is a system of moral principles. They affect how people make decisions and lead their lives.

Ethics is concerned with what is good for individuals and society and is also described as moral philosophy.

The term is derived from the Greek word *ethos* which can mean custom, habit, character or disposition.

Ethics covers the following topics:

- How to live a good life.
- Our rights and responsibilities.
- The language of right and wrong.
- Moral decisions – what is good and bad?

A person who knows the difference between right and wrong and chooses right is moral. A person whose morality is reflected in his willingness to do the right thing – even if it is hard or dangerous – is ethical. Ethics are moral values in action.

Virtue and acting virtuously is about thinking and doing what is right and avoiding what is wrong. Virtue is also defined as a personality trait; an inclination to act, desire, and feel that which involves the exercise of good judgment and leads to a recognizable human excellence and doing well in life. We are not born with a fixed character. It is, we suppose, partly up to ourselves what character traits we acquire. Those which help us to make the most of our lives are the virtues; without them, we cannot prosper.

Children are potentially (if not actually) moral subjects. The aim is to instil a moral responsibility for themselves. This practice is considered important in positively contributing to a child's good character and self-esteem. It is our own responsibility in seeing to it that children are taught the meaning of being a good character by practicing the virtues i.e., the ability to *know* what is good, to *want* what is good, and to *do* good.

THE VIRTUES THAT WILL BE INTRODUCED IN THE COURSE

- HONESTY
- TRUST
- FRIENDSHIP
- COURAGE
- LOYALTY
- KINDNESS AND CARING
- OWNERSHIP
- PERSEVERANCE
- GRATITUDE
- PATIENCE
- HAVING A SENSE OF PURPOSE
- DOING SOMETHING MAGNIFICENT

THE TEACHER'S AND PUPIL'S NOTES

Each subject of virtue to discuss has teacher's notes and a copy of the pupil's notes. The teacher's notes provide an easy to understand philosophical background to each subject of virtue. Teachers have the option to introduce these deeper points to the pupils if they think it appropriate.

The pupil's notes have been kept concise for ease of learning and understanding.

On each of the pupil's subject of virtue page, pupils should first read the notes then there are questions for them to discuss with one another and then to share their opinions with the teacher. The questions are the more important components of the course.

The pupil's pages need to be photocopied and distributed. The pupil's pages have been limited to a single sheet of paper for ease of photocopying or printing off.

The pupil's questions mostly ask what *'you'* would do in a given circumstances and moral dilemmas. These questions are asking for the attitudes of each individual pupil. However, one study cautioned that teachers need to be aware of the possibility that some pupils may sometimes be answering questions in a way that they perceive to be socially acceptable answers, rather than what they truly believed.

The pupils should discuss their understanding of each subject of virtue and discuss the possible answers to the questions with their fellow classmates who share the same table. It is suggested to do it this way as psychological research found that peer interaction is a powerful means to promote pupil learning and development. To emphasise this particular point, another piece of research found that pupils enjoyed and engaged with this peer-to-peer exercise, which brought out a surprisingly high level of moral language, understanding and moral subtlety.

There is an extra exercise at the end of the course which is a pupil's month's diary. Pupils can record any virtuous action they did that month and perhaps discuss it.

Aristotle believed that moral virtue comes about as a result of habit; habitually performing virtuous acts can become second nature. Aristotle concludes that whether or not we can lead a good life depends a great deal on the habits we form when we are young, in our childhood and early adulthood.

By pupils recording their good actions in the diary, it would be a reminder of what they have achieved; that they may be more likely to remember and repeat these good and positive deeds.

It could be a good idea for the teacher to ask the pupils what they had entered in their diary at the end of the month and to talk about it. Perhaps repeating the exercise for another few months is an option.

Finally, there are resources available for those teachers who wish to go into more depth on the subjects introduced in the course.

For more detailed resources on character building involving ethics, morality and virtues, go to the Jubilee Centre for Character and Virtues (2013b) *A Framework for Character Education in Schools*, Birmingham: Jubilee Centre for Character and Virtues, University of Birmingham. **Website http://www.jubileecentre.ac.uk/**

PUPIL'S INTRODUCTION TO THE COURSE ON ETHICS, MORALITY AND VIRTUES

What you will be learning in this course is all about how to be a really good person; to do good things and achieve the things you want to do in your life.

You will be learning about **ethics**, **morality** and the importance of **virtue**.

Ethics are rules based on ideas about what is accepted as good or bad behaviour. One example of good behaviour would be to often help people who are having difficulties. Bad behaviour would be things like stealing or murdering someone. **Ethics** is not only about taking particular courses of action but also about the goodness of yourself and others and what it means to live a good life.

Ethics tries to answer questions like:

- What actions are good? What actions are evil?
- How can we tell the difference?
- How should we make hard decisions that might help or hurt other people?
- How do our actions affect others?

A person who knows the difference between right and wrong and chooses right is a **moral** person. People who are **moral** is reflected in their willingness to do the right thing – even if it can be sometimes hard or dangerous.

Virtue is the action of doing what is right and avoiding what is wrong. Acting **virtuously** helps to make your life happier, and helps you to achieve good and great things that can benefit not only yourself but other people as well.

You will be learning about the **virtues** of:

HONESTY, TRUST, FRIENDSHIP, COURAGE, LOYALTY, KINDNESS AND CARING, OWNERSHIP, SENSE OF PURPOSE, PERSEVERANCE, GRATITUDE, PATIENCE, DOING SOMETHING MAGNIFICENT

THE VIRTUE OF HONESTY

This is a very deep and often a difficult and complex subject even for adults to understand and obviously more so for young children. However, this section emphasizes that telling the truth in the majority of cases is a very important and virtuous act. Honesty is a key factor in the development of a child's character. Truthfulness matters because it is necessary to support trust and co-operation, without which social life would be radically impoverished. But there can be cases where lying can sometimes do more good than harm.

On the pupil's page, the question regarding the giving of a pencil case as a prize is one example where there can be a choice to either tell the truth or tell a lie.

In the moral domain, the concern for others' wellbeing and the need to avoid harm could in certain cases motivate one to tell a lie in certain circumstances to promote social acceptance and friendship (e.g., "I really like your gift" or "You look great in that dress") rather than telling the blunt truth (e.g., "I do not like your gift" or "you look fat in that dress").

The question on protecting a friend or stranger from serious harm implies that lying in this case may be excusable.

Cheating is another form of dishonesty. Cheating can be defined as a hidden and deliberate way to break a rule in order to gain an advantage. Cheating can be an issue in the classroom but children need to be aware that it is always a bad choice. For example, children need to know that by cheating their way through spelling tests, they won't learn how to spell. If a child is under pressure to perform well in school, then there is the danger that they may resort to cheating as a means of achieving success.

It may also be excusable to lie if a person is under threat from someone who wants to seriously harm you. However, in the case of preventing a much lesser harm to yourself, the question is whether a child would lie in order to escape punishment from their teacher or parent for something they had done wrong.

There may be other cases where lying was kindly meant. There may be circumstances where lying did no harm or was doing less harm than telling the truth would have done.

Just such a case was when the British philosopher Sir Isaiah Berlin in his eighty sixth year, was interviewed about his views on death and dying. He said that he saw no reason to believe there is a world after death. He went on to say: his father had told him that he hoped that there was a future life. In fact, when he was dying, he asked me if I thought there was going to be life after death. I said that yes, I did. That was a lie because I did not want to tell him what I really believed. So I did not tell the truth, and I don't regret it. Since I believed that nothing would follow one's death, why should I cause a dying father pain?

The French philosopher Blaise Pascal, properly interpreted, got it exactly right: 'The first rule is to speak [only] the truth; the second is to speak with discretion'.

That said, young children have yet to have experience of life in such a way that would enable them to make these sophisticated moral judgements about where and when it may be more beneficial to lie in certain circumstances. Encouraging children to always tell the truth from an early age is clearly the best way forward.

THE VIRTUE OF HONESTY

It is very important not to lie and always tell the truth.

Honesty means telling the truth no matter what consequences you may face. Honest people do what they say they are going to do and never lie, cheat or steal.

If everyone in the world kept telling lies, you would not be able to believe anything anyone said. The world would not be a good place.

When you tell the truth people will respect you, and you will feel better about yourself.

People who cheat at tests by copying other people's work and claiming it was their own work are being dishonest. They also cheat themselves in a way because they don't make an honest attempt to learn as much as they can.

Being honest means you admit to doing something wrong, even if you'll get in trouble.

Honesty means you explain how a situation really happened. You are not being honest if you say something happened one way when it really happened another way.

QUESTIONS

- Why don't people always tell the truth?

- What kind of problems does dishonesty cause?

- Suppose you won a competition in your class and your teacher gave you a pencil case as a prize but you already had many pencil cases at home so you did not like the prize. If the teacher asked you if you liked your prize, should you lie and say yes to be polite to your teacher and not to hurt her feelings, or should you tell the truth and say no, 'I do not like my prize? Do you think there can be times when it could be unkind to be honest?

- Can you think of other circumstances where you could choose to lie, and that might be better than telling the truth? For example, suppose your friend came to your house to hide from some people who did not like him and wanted to harm him. If these people knocked on your door and asked if your friend was with you, should you tell a lie and say he was not in the house with you?

- Suppose you had a test at school and you cheated by copying the answers from the person sitting next to you. Why is this a bad thing to do?

- Can you think of a time when you were tempted to do something that was not honest but changed your mind in the end?

- Can you think of any examples of dishonesty you really dislike?

- How do you feel when people have been dishonest with you?

- How important is it to you that your friends be honest?

TEACHER'S NOTES

THE VIRTUE OF TRUST

Trusting someone means that you think they are reliable, you have confidence in them and you feel safe with them physically and emotionally. Trust is something that two people in a relationship can build together when they decide to trust each other. Trust can also be defined as a belief in something or a confident expectation about something.

Life runs more smoothly when people trust you. Without trust, social life would be impossible. Trust allows us to form relationships with people and to depend on them.

There are three basic things that trust does in the lives of people: it makes social life predictable, it creates a sense of <u>community</u>, and it makes it easier for people to work together. Success can be achieved through trust while working on projects that rely on each individual's contribution.

Trust is important because trust that is justified contributes to the foundation of a good society. It helps people to thrive through healthy cooperation with others and to be morally mature human beings.

One study identified trust as an indicator of healthy child development and stable adult relationships.

Trust is considered as an important ingredient of a number of other virtues discussed in the course: honesty, friendship, loyalty and courage.

Being trustworthy is considered to be a virtue. A trustworthy person is deserving of trust and can be relied on as being honest, dependable and reliable.

Reliability is often associated with trust and trustworthiness but philosophers believe there is a distinction between these three. Trust, is to have faith and confidence in the intentions and actions of others – to believe that they will do the right thing. To be trustworthy, a person has to demonstrate by words and acts that people can trust them. A reliable person is usually predictable such as a dependable plumber, a responsible babysitter, people you know who have a history of not letting you down.

We have no option but to trust people that most of us have no control over, who perform services for our benefit and well-being – such as doctors, the police, the government.

Trust is important, but it can also be dangerous. Trust usually involves being optimistic, rather than pessimistic; that the trusted person will do something for us (or for others perhaps), but that can makes us vulnerable. Because of this, trust can sometimes be a gamble especially when you can never be sure of the actions of the person you trust. The person who trusts someone must be able to accept that by trusting, he or she can be betrayed. If this happens, trust is lost and it is very hard to regain.

Despite this, most good relationships are built on mutual trust and respect. Trustworthiness is admirable, something to be aspired to: it is a virtue in the everyday sense.

THE VIRTUE OF TRUST

Trust is an important thing in life. It affects your relationship with other people; your friends, your family. Life would be very difficult if we could not trust other people or other people could not trust us.

Having trust in someone means that you think they are honest and reliable and you have complete confidence in them and being able to count on them not to let you down. Trust is important for people in a relationship such as the one you have with your best friends and your family. Having trust in one another can build a strong and happy relationship. You trust that your family is always looking out for you and has your best interests at heart and are always there to give you help and support. We also have to trust people that most of us have no control over. These are people who perform services for our benefit and well-being such as doctors, the police, or the government.

When you want someone to trust you, you need to show that you are trustworthy.

Being trustworthy means:

- Being reliable; doing what you say you'll do.
- Having the courage to do the right thing.
- Being honest.
- Not deceiving, cheating or stealing.
- Being loyal; standing by your friends.
- Keeping private information private.

If you are untrustworthy or someone is untrustworthy to you, it is important to remember that when trust is lost and it is very hard to regain.

QUESTIONS

- Do you consider yourself a trustworthy person? In what way are you a trustworthy person?

- How important is trust in your relationships with friends, family, and teachers?

- What does trust have to do with honesty? How would these relationships be affected if they found you had not been truthful?

- What is his/her best quality that makes you friends? Do you think that is a trustworthy quality? Why do you trust them?

- Have you ever broken a promise to someone? How do you think it made that person feel?

- What might cause your parents to stop trusting you?

- Do you think that trusting people may sometimes be a risk? Why?

THE VIRTUE OF FRIENDSHIP

Many studies have demonstrated the importance of friendship in a child's life. At least half of children with signs of emotional or behavioural problems have no friends.

Friendships contribute significantly to the development of social skills, such as being sensitive to other people's point of view, learning the rules of conversation. They also help define both self and self-worth.

Friends also have a powerful influence on a child's positive and negative school performance and may also help to encourage, or discourage, deviant behaviours, such as delinquency or drug use. Compared to children who lack friends, children with "good" friends have higher self-esteem. They are less likely to be lonely and act more pro-socially. They are able to cope with life stresses and normal transitions and are also less victimized by peers. Interestingly, children with friends of both sexes, as a group, are more well-adjusted and have greater social skills than children who have only friends of the same sex.

It has been suggested that there are three key ingredients of children's friendship formation: (1) openness, (2) similarity, and (3) shared fun.

Aristotle wrote extensively about friendship in his *Nicomachean Ethics*. He believed that friendship is indispensable for human life and happiness. He also proposed that it is at the very least a relationship of goodwill between individuals who reciprocate that goodwill. He also thought that true friends, are mirrors to each other. An ancient Greek politician Cicero echoed Aristotle when he said: "A friend is, as it were, a second self."

Essentially, a good friend will always be your friend and stick by you in good times and in bad times. Trust is also considered as an important factor in friendship. The virtue of loyalty is also considered to be a factor in a friendship. Loyalty strengthens the bond between friends, increases the trust between them and you know you can always open up to that friend. All of which is needed for a friendship to grow and sustain.

THE VIRTUE OF FRIENDSHIP

Having good friends is absolutely brilliant!

It's not much fun being on your own. With friends you can have a lot more fun doing the things you both like to do.

It's great to know you have a friend to hang out with when you get out of school.

Having friends makes you feel really good about yourself and your life can be a happy one when you have a friend.

One of the ways that friendship make us feel good is having someone else to talk to. This is important because it makes us feel like we are not alone.

A good friendship means caring for each other's safety and wellbeing. Good friends help each other solve problems.

A good friend is someone you can trust and share things with. You can talk to them about your future plans, worries or problems which you wouldn't think of sharing with anyone else. You can help your friend in the same way if they had something that was worrying them

A good friend doesn't go round telling other people what you have asked them to be private. Trust is earned over time but can be lost with a broken promise.

Being a good friend means you respect each other's opinion. You listen and try to understand their point of view even if you don't always agree with them.

A good friend will always be your friend and stick by you in good times and in bad times.

You can have different friends who share your different interests. Best friends are special. Most people would say that they are friendly with lots of people but they only have a few close friends. This will always be the case even when you have grown up.

QUESTIONS

- Think about your own friend – what makes them a good friend?

- Have you ever helped a friend when they really needed help? What happened?

- If you told your best friend a secret, what would you think if they told someone else?

- Would you tell your friend if you thought he was acting wrongly?

- If you saw one of your classmates all alone in the playground, would you ask them to join the person or group you were friendly with?

- Should you help others even when they are not your friends?

- Has a friend ever let you down?

- What makes friends different from your family?

THE VIRTUE OF COURAGE

Courage is a display of: mental and emotional strength in facing difficulty, adversity, danger, fear and possessing restraint and tolerance. It can also include aspects of perseverance; setting realistic but challenging goals for oneself and in persisting with these under adversity.

Aristotle considered courage as an important virtue. In his Nichomachean Ethics, he makes the point that one should establish the middle ground between two extremes. So in courage, he believes in avoiding cowardice such as letting people take advantage over you on the one hand and recklessness on the other such as putting yourself in extreme danger with the high risk of being seriously harmed. Aristotle further suggested that those who tend towards risky behaviour should consider how they can learn greater respect for the real risks and dangers of a situation. Courage therefore requires using practical reason towards making a sound judgement in a dangerous situation and not giving in to excessive or irrational emotion.

The Scottish philosopher David Hume asserted that: "Courage defends us, but cowardice lays us open to every attack"

The German philosopher Friedrich Nietzsche wrote: "A heart full of courage and cheerfulness needs a little danger from time to time, or the world gets unbearable."

The French philosopher Comte-Sponville stated that: "the capacity to overcome fear "is always more valued than cowardice or faintheartedness"

Courage is a physical act but it can also be a moral act. Moral courage is the ability to act rightly in the face of popular opposition, discouragement, or personal loss.

The Italian philosopher Thomas Aquinas holds courage as being primarily about endurance, not aggression. He believed that the major act of courage is to stand immovable in the midst of dangers rather than to attack them.

Perhaps a good example of needing to be courageous in a school setting is where a pupil is the victim of bullying and needs the courage to stand up and challenge that bully.

Bullying can be a major issue that can seriously affect the lives of some schoolchildren. According to the UK website of Anti-Bullying Alliance, 40% of young people were bullied in the last 12 months and that 24% of children bullied most days are also most likely to be kept off school by their parents.

It is possible a display of courage could in some way lessen the harm that bullying does. For example, it has been suggested that many bullies are afraid themselves and when confronted with their victim's courage in facing up to them, they may stop.

THE VIRTUE OF COURAGE

We usually feel comfortable and don't fear anything when things are safe. But there will be times when you do not feel comfortable and safe. That is when you need courage.

Courage is about doing something you are afraid to do. Having the courage to do that can mean you saying "this might work so I'll try it"

You need to have courage when you try something new that you think will be very difficult even if you might fail. If you did fail, having courage would be saying "I'll try again tomorrow."

It takes courage to admit your mistakes and try to learn from them.

Courage is being able to speak up for something you believe in.

The next time you are afraid to do something but you know it is the right thing to do, just do it. See how it makes you feel.

It is important to be courageous but there may be times when you are not courageous enough and times when you can be too courageous.

Not being courageous enough can mean that you give in to people who threaten or bully you and you don't do anything to stand up and defend yourself.

There may be times where it is better not to be too courageous. Being too courageous is when you put yourself in great danger. For example, you are at the seaside. You want to try and rescue your dog that has been swept out to sea. If you did go into the sea hoping to rescue your dog, you might be swept out to sea yourself and you could drown.

So the aim is to try and find the 'middle ground' between being too cowardly and being too brave.

QUESTIONS

- What is something courageous that you've done? How did you feel after you did it?

- A time when I wish I had more courage was…?

- Can you remember a story that you have read where a person had courage?

- What are some things you would like to do in your life that takes courage?

- Would you have the courage to help your friend who is being bullied?

- Is a passerby who rushes into a burning building to save someone more courageous than a professional fire-fighter?

- Do you think being fearful of something helps? Would we be better off if we were not capable of feeling fear? What might happen?

THE VIRTUE OF LOYALTY

The American philosopher Josiah Royce defined the virtue of loyalty as "the willing and practical and thoroughgoing devotion of a person to a cause"

Loyalty is considered to be a meaningful virtue in terms of relationships between colleagues. Loyalty can be seen as the tie that binds groups of people together in pursuit of their cause. For the individual, loyalty can mean that person's sense of identity and belonging to his or her group.

It has been suggested that if we could not count on the loyalties of others or give them our loyalty, social life would not only be bleak but impossible.

Loyalty is one of those virtues that enable us to realize more fully the human potential within us. Indeed, individuals might never develop as a person if they lived their lives in isolation. The individual develops his personality in relationships with others.

When loyalty is given to a friend or a team member who is having a difficult time, the loyalty given could be counted on being reciprocated if ever that person found themselves in similarly difficult circumstances.

Loyalty is an important virtue in team building. Team building starts when people identify with the team. How well people connect with the team determines how well the team bonds. A sense of loyalty and trust is powerful and crucial in shaping the team. Creating this bond moves a team from good to almost unstoppable. And from loyalty comes a sense of purpose.

A study found that teachers who are loyal to the school and the head are willing to put additional effort to help children achieve at a higher level. The study also found that teachers who are loyal to each other build the cohesion necessary for successful cooperation and interaction.

Considering loyalty as a virtue can sometimes run in to difficulties. What of an individual's decision to be loyal to an evil cause for example a Nazi party member's oath of loyalty to Hitler? In this context loyalty can be perverted by an obsession or blind fanaticism with wrongdoing. Cases like this are not loyalty at all; it is a perversion of loyalty. Loyalty doesn't defend malicious intentions. A friend who steals may not be a bad person, but a person who made a bad choice. Separating that one wrong act from the friend allows a person to remain loyal to that friend without changing his or her own values and interests.

THE VIRTUE OF LOYALTY

Being loyal means remaining faithful to such things as your family, friends, your team, your school, your country.

With loyalty, you build relationships that last a long time.

Being loyal to your friend means you supporting them not only when things are going well but also when they are going through bad times.

You remain loyal to your friend by not going around telling other people anything that your friend wanted you to keep secret.

Football fans show loyalty to the team they support even when their team is doing very badly. Loyalty can be important when you are part of a team. Loyalty to one another in the team helps the team to have a greater chance in achieving its goals. People who are members of a team such as mountain rescue teams and lifeboat crews have a strong sense of loyalty and trust in one another.

Showing loyalty to other people in your team means forming a relationship that is a sort of glue which sticks your team together and makes it stronger and more successful.

Good team leaders try to make sure everyone feels included; this would encourage loyalty to the team. The loyalty of every team member is important for the survival of the group as a whole.

It is important to keep in mind that loyalty does not mean that you must be loyal to an evil cause or a bad person. That is the opposite of loyalty because it supports something that is totally unacceptable or unreasonable.

QUESTIONS

- Have you ever played on a sports team? Would you try to score a goal for the other team? Why not?
- In what ways can you be loyal to:
    - Your friends?
    - Your family?
    - Your team?
    - Your school?
    - Your country?
- If one of your friends did something wrong like stealing something from a shop, should you still stay loyal to your friend?

KINDNESS AND CARING

"I believe that if we stop to think, it is clear that our very survival, even today, depends upon the acts and kindness of so many people. Right from the moment of our birth, we are under the care and kindness of our parents; later in life, when facing the sufferings of disease and old age, we are again dependent on the kindness of others."

The Dalai Lama

Kindness and caring for others is considered a <u>virtue</u>, and is recognized as a <u>value</u> in many cultures and religions.

Showing kindness and caring to others basically shares three main definitions:

- Compassion – sympathetic pity and concern for the sufferings or misfortunes of others.
- Altruism – the quality of unselfish concern for the well-being of others. But the giver of the kindness can also benefit from being kind and caring themselves. A large body of research has established an association between kindness and well-being.
- Caring – is someone or something that shows kindness and concern for others. A person who is concerned about others and who does kind things for them.

Aristotle defines kindness as being "helpfulness towards someone in need, not in return for anything, nor for the advantage of the helper himself, but for that of the person helped"

The Greek writer Aesop said: 'No act of kindness, no matter how small, is ever wasted.'

The importance of showing kindness is considered to be a very important aspect to life and much has been written on the importance of children acquiring the habit of showing kindness to others.

A large body of research has established an association between kindness and well-being. Indeed, we might even expect helping others to produce more happiness than helping yourself.

A sense of community is created when people are kind to those who need help.

Humans tend to be caring people. If we see an elderly person fall in the street, we rush to help them without having to think about it. People can disagree over many things but nearly everyone would agree that building a children's hospital would be a good idea.

THE VIRTUE OF KINDNESS AND CARING

Being kind and caring is a virtue that means feeling and showing concern to other people, and willing to help them when they have difficulties. Caring and kindness can also apply to animals and other creatures like helping a spider or bug out of your house instead of squashing it. You can also be kind and caring for the environment such as picking up litter or planting something new.

You never know what that little bit of kindness will mean to someone's day.

It's good to be kind and caring to others because it can make you feel happy as well!

Kindness is doing good things for people you know without expecting anything in return. You can show kindness to strangers: a kind act may be a way of making a new friend.

There are many ways you can be kind to other people. You can help a friend out who is feeling a bit sad. If someone you know is ill, you can go and see them and try to cheer them up.

If you know an old person who needs some help, you could do things such as doing the shopping for them. Older people who live on their own can get very lonely and some of them don't have many people visiting them, so just calling round to talk with them is a great thing to do.

Disabled people sometimes struggle to do things in life we take for granted. Disabled people like to remain independent but you may see them struggle a bit trying to do something – then you could offer to help them.

It doesn't always have to be a big act of kindness – small things count just as much such as giving a smile to someone.

QUESTIONS

- Do you think it is important to help other people who have problems, not just family and friends?

- How did you feel when you helped or cared for other people? What did you do for them?

- How would you cheer up a person you know is feeling a bit sad?

- What is the kindest thing anyone has done for you? How did it make you feel?

- Do you think it is just as important to care for yourself?

- Do you think doing an act of kindness to someone will affect how they treat others? If so, how?

- If you were not really interested in other people's problems, do you think this would be a poor choice and why?

OWNERSHIP

Ownership, in its most basic form, constitutes a relationship between a person and some other entity that is acknowledged and respected by other people.

Owned entities can take many forms—objects, land, ideas, even living entities like pets, or at certain points in history, other people.

Ownership can be considered to be a virtue. One aspect of ownership is its connection to the virtue of generosity; we can choose to loan what we own to another person who would benefit from the loan such as loaning a tool to a neighbour so they can do some badly needed work.

It has been suggested that ownership serves as a key factor in accelerating the growth and development of an individual.

Ownership is a moral right to directly control something you own. Moral rights mean the things you own cannot be taken away from you without your consent.

Ownership also introduces the notion of autonomy, which is the ability to make one's own decisions about the object you own without being controlled by anyone else; having a sense of independence.

The ancient Greek philosopher Aristotle (in his Politics) proclaimed that private property was necessary in order to achieve individual moral development and thus social harmony.

The German philosopher Hegel stated: Property is not merely material acquisition — it is central to an individual's assertion of identity and personality. Property is an expression of self and the locus of an individual's claim to rights, since it is through property that one can say "this is mine," a claim that others respect. Property is the "embodiment of personality,"

We tend to enjoy owning certain things because they have a particular function; they make possible certain activities and pleasures.

There are personal and emotional aspects when a person gives sentimental value to an object they own. The loss of this object would be harmful to the person and lead to a feeling of sadness.

It has been found that children who create something themselves see it as a more meaningful form of ownership rather than owning something that has been given a present.

Ownership is not only concerned with owning an object, it is also concerned with owning an idea. Good and original ideas serve as a signal to one's prestige and creativity and is therefore valuable. With any original good ideas, there may be a danger that other people could 'steal' the idea and call it their own. Understanding how children reason about ownership of ideas can inform our understanding of how to motivate them to create and ultimately pursue their own ideas, as well as develop their unique ideas in collaborations with others.

Interestingly, The National Literacy Trust did a survey in 2011 on the subject of children's book ownership and its relation to reading enjoyment, attitudes, behaviour and attainment. They discovered that:

Although other factors such as socio-economic status and gender may have a part to play in children and young people's relationship to books and reading, the relationship between book ownership and reading attitudes and abilities is consistently strong. When compared to peers who do not have books of their own, children who own books:

- enjoy reading more
- read more books
- read more frequently
- read for longer lengths of time when they do read
- have more books in the home
- read more of every kind of material not just books
- are more likely to have been bought a book as a presen
- are more likely to have ever visited a library or bookshop
- have more positive attitudes to reading
- find it easier to find books that interest them
- have higher attainment

The pupil's question about finding a mobile phone. Possible answers could be:

- As someone has lost the phone, you are only the guardian of it while you try to find a way to find the owner.
- If it is impossible to find the owner, then you can claim ownership.

Who owns the pot question. Two possible answers.

- Peter owns it because Joe has taken some of his clay without permission.
- According to the opinion of British philosopher John Locke, Joe owns it because he has made something from his own labour.

The owner destroying a work of art question. Despite this being a regrettable act, the owner is legally entitled to do as he pleases. So the question is whether there should there be a rule of law that forbids the owner of a valuable piece of historically important art to destroy it?

OWNERSHIP

Somebody gave me a book as a gift and said it was mine to keep.

I now own this book, there are many books like it but this one is mine.

There are things you are allowed to do with a book or other objects that belong to you that you cannot do with objects that belong to someone else.

Because it is my book, I am free to decide what I want to do with it. If I read it myself and I think it is a really interesting book, I could be generous and loan the book to someone else who might be interested in reading it. I could also decide to give my book to someone else as a gift and by doing this, they now own the book.

If I bought a bicycle, then the bicycle belongs to me but a person who steals one is a thief.

If you have a good idea for a story and write it down, then you own that idea. It would be wrong for someone to steal your story and claim it was their own idea.

We usually like to own things that make it possible to do the things we enjoy doing such as owning a tennis racquet so we can play tennis or owning a musical instrument so we can play music.

QUESTIONS

- If you gave your book as a gift to someone else and then decided I wanted to have the book back, would the person I gave the book to now have to give it back to me?

- What is the favourite thing that you own? Why is it your favourite?

- How would you feel if somebody stole something that you owned?

- If you made a work of art, do you think there is a difference between owning something you have made yourself and an object that someone has given you as a present?

- If you find an expensive mobile phone in the park, can you now own it or should you try to find a way to find the owner first?

- Peter and Joe are making clay pots. Each has their own lump of clay. Without Peter knowing, Joe takes some extra clay from Peter's clay and makes another new pot. Who owns Joe's new pot?

- Can people who own a valuable and historical work of art destroy it if they want to? If not, why not?

THE VIRTUE OF GRATITUDE

Gratitude is a virtue that promotes a positive emotional state. From the perspectives of moral philosophy and theology, gratitude is seen as a human strength that enhances one's personal and relational well-being and is beneficial for society as a whole.

The three major components of gratitude are: (a) a warm sense of appreciation for somebody or something, (b) a sense of goodwill toward that person or thing, and (c) a disposition to act that flows from appreciation and goodwill.

As a virtue, gratitude stems from the perception that one has experienced a positive outcome that has been intentionally provided by another person. But gratitude can also be shown to something that is impersonal such as appreciating the natural wonders of the world or non-human sources such as animals or God.

Gratitude is not only something that follows from receiving help from others but also by continually appreciating the positive aspects of life. Gratitude also helps build trust in social relationships . In addition, studies have argued that gratitude promotes positive effect, more satisfying relationships, and improved coping with stress.

The ancient Roman philosopher Seneca suggested that "Those who are incapable of gratitude live in vain; they can never be satisfied, fulfilled or happy."

Gratitude can also be understood to mean that one 'counts one's blessings.'

There is presently a growing interest in the area of gratitude in the younger generation

The American Wall Street Journal published an article about raising children with a sense of gratitude. The article cited studies showing that children who count their blessings reap concrete benefits, including greater life satisfaction and a better attitude about school.

When children recognize that the things they own and the opportunities they have come from someone other than themselves, it helps them develop a healthy understanding of how interdependent we all are — and they may be more inclined to treat others with genuine respect. It's a simple principle: gratitude fosters stronger, more positive and more genuine relationships. It can also promote a sense of well-being.

A recent study concluded that pondering the circumstances in one's life for which one is grateful appears to be a common way of coping with both acute and chronic stressful life events.

It seems clear that just saying thank you may be beyond just simple manners.

THE VIRTUE OF GRATITUDE

Showing gratitude to someone means that you thank them for a good act they have done for you; it means a readiness to show appreciation. For example, "I'd like to thank you for helping me to carry a lot of shopping."

Saying thank you is a good thing to do for everybody.

Saying thank you to someone increases good feelings for the person being thanked; they feel appreciated. Saying thank you also increases your own good feelings. Thanking people can not only make it more likely they'll also be grateful to others, but also you are more likely to show the same kindness to someone else.

Gratitude is not only being grateful to other people who help us. Gratitude can also be shown towards things you appreciate in your life such as enjoying walks in the country with all the plants and animals and birds you may see on the way. Gratitude is also being thankful for the good things you have; things you may often take for granted, like having a home to live in, a bed to sleep in, and enough food so you don't feel hungry all the time.

Being grateful for what you have is better than being jealous of what another person has or wanting a lot of things that you don't have.

QUESTIONS

- What are some things in your life you are most grateful for?

- What are your special gifts, talents and likes? Which are you most grateful for?

- What do you think would be the benefits of acknowledging the good things in your life more frequently?

- Do you often think about the things you don't have rather than acknowledging the things you do have?

- If you helped someone in difficulty, they will probably thank you but you can also thank them. Can you think of a reason why you could also thank them?

- A poor homeless person is having to sleep rough on the streets at night. Should they be grateful for what they have?

- If you were nearly drowning in the sea and rescued by a lifeguard, does he deserve gratitude even though it was his job and duty to try and save you?

THE VIRTUE OF PERSEVERANCE

In 2015, the UK Department of Education recognized the importance of encouraging the teaching of character development traits in schools that included perseverance as an important feature in enabling pupils to leave school more "fully rounded" and "better equipped to meet the challenges of employment and future life." Teaching awareness of the virtue of perseverance to younger children is just as important. Perseverance has been found to be a contributor to individual success in a variety of settings, as well as throughout an individual's life span.

Perseverance is an important factor in our own personal and professional lives where it can be the case that we often don't achieve what we could in our personal or professional lives because we simply don't persevere enough. Perseverance has been found to be a major predictor of long-term success. When disappointment or boredom signals to others that it is time to change trajectory and cut losses, the individual who perseveres stays the course.

The first aspect of perseverance is being optimistic about what can be accomplished and to accept the fact that failure is a necessary part of life; to persist in the face of the array of challenges and obstacles encountered throughout schooling and life.

Studies have found that although intelligence is a strong predictor of achievement, it does not always translate into achievement; perseverance is as least as crucial as intelligence.

People who overcome obstacles to reach their goals must some-times develop new approaches and techniques or new ways to solve problems, and these newly acquired skills can be beneficial in subsequent undertakings.

A core mindset to attain in developing responses to situations that supports perseverance is knowing "My ability and competence grow with my effort."

The ancient Greek philosopher Plato considered perseverance as a form of courage; being able to persevere through all emotions, like suffering, pleasure, and fear.

Importantly, children need opportunities to take on "optimally challenging" goals that, to the child, are worthy of pursuit. Children who persevere can grow to know how to remain engaged over the long haul and how to deploy new strategies for moving forward effectively.

Children can learn to see that initially finding tasks to be difficult not as personal failing but as an important "bump in the road" on the way to success.

DANGERS OF EXCESSES IN PERSEVERANCE

An excess of perseverance could be said to be a form of stubbornness; trying the same thing over and over again, even when it doesn't work. One principle is that children find goals worthy of pursuit when they are "optimally challenging"—they require some perseverance to attain, but not so much that they seem overwhelming or impossible.

No one wants their child to be someone who gives up easily, but it is also important to be strategic about when to call it a day.

It may not always be productive to persevere in the face of challenge. For example, persevering to accomplish goals that are not essential, unimportant to the child, or in some way inappropriate for the child can potentially induce stress, anxiety, and distraction, and have detrimental impacts on a child's psychological well being.

Aristotle's recommendation that one should seek to find the middle ground may be relevant here.

The middle ground would be between not persevering enough and being too perseverant in trying to do work that is not in line with one's interests, values, or goals.

THE VIRTUE OF PERSEVERANCE

What is perseverance?

Perseverance is the ability to stick it out when trying to learn or do something new and not give up – to keep going when things are tough.

Even though it feels so hard when you are working through a challenge, perseverance keeps pushing you through to your goal and to the good feeling that comes with knowing you did your best.

You don't have to be the smartest kid in the class; if you persevere, you can often reach your goals.

Learning how to play a musical instrument is one example of needing perseverance. Learning to play an instrument is hard but by putting the hours in and dedicating yourself to improving your skills, you'll nurture a sense of achievement which is pretty hard to beat.

There may be times when even your best plans fail but that should not make you give up every time. The author of the Harry Potter stories, J K Rowling had her book turned down by 12 publishers before one agreed to publish her book. If she had lacked perseverance and given up after all those rejections, then we would not have been able to read her very popular and well-liked books.

Sometimes we work hard and don't meet our goals, but knowing we did the best we could do gives us a sense of pride and self confidence. If you encounter difficulties, identify them and work out a solution, in other words, persevere!

Although perseverance is all about not giving up, sometimes you'll try and do your best but there may be times when you think it might be better to move on to a different goal. Trying the same thing over and over again, even when it doesn't work may sometimes be not a good thing to do.

QUESTIONS

- If you don't get it right first time, should you stop trying?
- Do you think people fail because they give up too easily?
- Do you remember a mistake you made? What did you learn from that mistake?
- Do you remember a time when you kept trying even though you felt like giving up?
- What motivated you to keep going?
- What sort of thing would make it difficult for you to continue?
- What achievements are you most proud of?
- How did you feel when you had accomplished your task?

THE VIRTUE OF PATIENCE

Patience is considered by many to be a virtue.

There are several types of patience, including patience in the face of irritation, patience in the face of boredom, patience in the face of misfortune, and, most difficult of all, patience in the face of suffering.

Patience allows us to consider things more thoughtfully – before deciding to act or think too quickly. The German philosopher Friedrich Nietzsche suggested that good judgement often requires and is learned through patience-by taking our time before judging.

Patience can often be essential to daily life—and might be key to a happier one. Having patience means being able to wait calmly in the face of frustration or adversity, and where this happens, we have the opportunity to practice it. When you learn and practice patience you don't get as angry, stressed or overwhelmed.

Research has found that a degree of patience can reduce stress levels. Patience can also result in better decision making. Take the time to assess the situation, see the big picture, and weigh any pros and cons. The chances of making a big mistake lessen because you avoid making it in haste. Patience can also be similar to, or an exercise of, self-control.

Consider the kindness, compassion, and generosity needed to develop meaningful friendships. It seems quite unlikely that one could attain these things through choosing only quickly-gained ends.

Rather than weaken us, patience frees us from frustration and its ills, delivers us to the present moment, and affords us the time and perspective to think, do, and say the right things. In other words, patience is largely a matter of confidence, or trust, or faith. It has also been suggested that patience supports the development of other moral strengths and virtues such as courage, justice, love, and hope.

However, there are some who argue that patience can be a vice rather than a virtue; good does not always come to those who wait.

There will be times when good things also come to those who *take action, commit, put in the work, persist, and persevere.* People who boldly go out to seize their own good can sometimes fare rather better than those who patiently await its arrival.

Perhaps we should not be patient in circumstances in which action is urgently needed; there is not always time to take our time.

It seems the patient person needs not only to know the right way to do the right thing in exercising patience in a particular circumstance, but also to be someone who does not indiscriminately exercise patience in all situations.

THE VIRTUE OF PATIENCE

Patience is "waiting without getting upset." Some things just take time—like travelling from one place to another, standing in a queue or learning something new. A patient person responds to these situations with a positive outlook and attitude.

When you learn and practice patience you don't get as angry, stressed or overwhelmed.

Patience is a necessary part of life. Instead of getting frustrated when you face a difficult situation, patience helps you respond the right way—without getting upset or losing your temper. You need to see things and situations in a positive light to make your life happier and to get that positivity, you need to be patient.

Patience can give you the opportunity to wait until you've learned as much as you can before you decide what action to take.

 Patience helps us avoid making impulsive decisions and helps with self-control and calmness.

Patience helps us to become more sympathetic towards people who may be disabled or disadvantaged in some way who cannot move or think as quickly as you such as trying to get on a bus. These are the times when with patience, you can think beyond your own needs and place the needs of others above your own.

Sure enough, good things really do come to those who wait. However, there will be times when you need to be more decisive.

You may decide to play the waiting game; being patient, sitting still, and expecting something to happen. But sometimes there's no virtue in waiting around and hoping for something to happen. There may be circumstances when you may need to commit to and take action to create the right circumstances to achieve your dreams and goals.

Remember that all the major scientific discoveries had lots of hard work and patience behind them.

QUESTIONS

- How do you think patience can help you in life?
- Can you remember times when if you had been a bit more patient, things would have worked out better?
- Can you remember times when you had to be patient and wait for things to happen?
- Can you remember any times when you think you missed important opportunities to act while you waited for everything to be in place?
- What do you think about people who are not patient such as those who often complain, jump queues, are aggressive, and just jump to conclusions rather than thinking things through?

THE VIRTUE OF HAVING A SENSE OF PURPOSE

Having a sense of purpose has been regarded as a virtue in virtually all eras and cultures.

Purpose is a moral virtue that potentially will contribute to the achievement of happiness and flourishing.

There appears to be a consensus growing among researchers that having a sense of purpose represents a stable and generalized intention to accomplish something that is at once meaningful to the self and leads to productive engagement with some aspect of the world beyond the self.

Other research has shown that having a sense of purpose is really important for not only our happiness but also for our emotional wellbeing and development. Purpose keeps us motivated, gives us energy and helps us cope with any problems or difficult circumstances that come up. Purpose is also about recognising and fulfilling our highest potential, allowing us to be our best and give our best to others.

Having a sense of purpose can be an important contributor to the young person's character development. Young people are happier when they have a sense of purpose in their lives.

As children grow older, their thinking will become more abstract and they will begin to question their identity and purpose in life. They will want to know who they are and who they are to be.

Researchers have found that a lack of a sense of purpose in young people can lead to early personal difficulties such as selfishness, lack of enthusiasm, depression, as well as social difficulties such as antisocial behaviour and unstable close relationships. It has also been found to lead to risky behaviours such as drug-taking.

Children who lack a sense of purpose typically are unmotivated and generally have low self-esteem.

Research has concluded that teachers should believe that every child in their class has a purpose and that they can succeed in that purpose. If you believe in them, they are more likely to believe in themselves.

THE VIRTUE OF HAVING A SENSE OF PURPOSE

Having a sense of purpose in life is the motivation that drives you toward a rewarding and enjoyable future. Having a sense of purpose in your life is a desire to achieve something that is important to you. It is also about recognising and fulfilling your highest potential, allowing you to be your best and give your best to others.

Your purpose may be about what you want to achieve or it may be more about what kind of person you want to be.

Purpose is about more than just ourselves – it's also about having a positive impact on the lives of others in some way, such as helping to improve the local community or the environment.

Having a purpose is a good thing but it needs you to be able to achieve realistic goals. In order to achieve these realistic goals, you need to discover what your own talents and strengths are.

Trying to achieve your goals give you that sense of meaning and purpose, a clear sense of direction. As you move toward to achieving your goals you feel happier and stronger. You feel more competent and confident in yourself and your abilities.

A sense of purpose in doing something helps you to stop complaining about negative things in your life and, rather, take control of your life and shape it the way you would like it to go. You make things happen.

QUESTIONS

- What aspects of your life are you most interested in?
- What sort of things do you love to do and what would you really like to do?
- What do you do that makes you feel really good about yourself?
- Have you ever done something that really absorbed you?
- If you could change some things in the world, what are the differences you would like to make?

DOING SOMETHING MAGNIFICENT!

The Austrian philosopher Otto Weininger held that: 'genius is the highest morality, and, therefore, it is everyone's duty'. By this he meant that one's major duty was to do something magnificent in one's life. Doing something magnificent would not only be a positive and highly satisfying thing to do but also a by-product of performing such an act would benefit other people and make their lives better.

Young people have an important role to play in making the world a better place.

The ancient Roman politician and lawyer Cicero refers doing something magnificent into the greatness of the task, the intention to realize it, and the determination to carry it through. He also says that patience is a requirement to embark on doing arduous tasks and perseverance in a well-considered plan of action.

The Italian philosopher Thomas Aquinas stated that magnificence belongs to the virtue of fortitude, or courage, because it regards the undertaking of great things and actions, and to persevere even when circumstances can make their realization arduous.

Creativity is an important component of genius and it is worth noting that there is recognition that creative people are not necessarily intellectually brilliant. Not all creativity needs to be a totally new idea. Geniuses have demonstrated the ability to recycle an idea and transform it into something else.

Even though different pupils might identify the same goals, they might have a different number of barriers to achieving that goal. It is also important to acknowledge that some pupils may be more talented and have an advantage over other pupils. It may also be worth bearing in mind that some pupils may have already faced a great deal of failure and others have not.

DOING SOMETHING MAGNIFICENT!

All of us have the ability to be a genius and be able to do something magnificent in our life. A genius is someone who has a very great ability or skill in a particular subject or activity. We are all good at doing something so it is possible for all of us to be geniuses!

Try to achieve something you passionately believe in. Make it possible to turn your own ideas in to something that will make a big difference to peoples' lives in a positive way

Even in a small way, you can contribute and make a difference to the world. For example, try thinking of things that can help improve the life of people who have problems. Think about the challenges or difficulties they face and think of how you can solve those problems.

That feeling of making a difference is ultimately what's most important for your own happiness and sense of achievement.

Doing something magnificent is often about problem solving. Find a problem you care about and think about ways of solving it.

Try not to let any obstacle stand in their way of doing something you strongly believe in. But you have to be realistic when taking on doing something magnificent. You cannot move mountains or teach a goldfish how to play the violin.

Doing something magnificent does not mean you have to do it all on your own. Your idea may need the help of others – good teamwork can also help to achieve magnificent results!

QUESTIONS ABOUT YOU

You may already be a genius! You have your own talents or skills that will enable you to achieve doing something magnificent! Think about the answers to the next four questions.

- What things can you do well without much effort?
- What things do others tell you that you are good at?
- What things do you always find the enthusiasm and energy for?
- What achievements are you proud of?

MORE QUESTIONS

- What magnificent things do you think you can do to make a big difference to your family, class, community, workplace, the world?
- Do you think you may need the help of others sometimes in order to achieve your goal or do you decide to do everything alone?
- Which of the virtues which you have learned in the course do you think you will need in order to achieve your goal?

DIARY FOR THE MONTH OF:

Was there anything that you did this month that matched any of the virtues listed below you have been learning and discussing?

If you did, why did you do it and what happened as a result?

HONESTY, TRUST, FRIENDSHIP, COURAGE, LOYALTY, KINDNESS AND CARING, OWNERSIP, GRATITUDE, PERSEVERANCE, PATIENCE, SENSE OF PURPOSE, DOING SOMETHING MAGNIFICENT.

BILIOGRAPHY

Adler MG, Fagley NS. Appreciation: individual differences in finding value and meaning as a unique predictor of subjective well-being. Journal of Personality. 2005 Feb;73(1):79-114.

Aristotle. Nicomachean ethics

Berkowitz, Marvin W, Ph.D.. Bier, Melinda C Ph.D. What Works In Character Education: A research-driven guide for educators Character Education Partnership University of Missouri-St. Louis February 2005.

Berkowitz, Marvin W and Melinda C. What works in character education. Bier Journal of Research in Character Education, 5(1), 2007, pp. 29–48

Blake, P. R., & Harris, P. L. (2011). Early representations of ownership. In H. Ross & O. Friedman (Eds.), Origins of ownership of property. New Directions for Child and Adolescent Development, 132, 39–51

Bommarito, N. Patience and Perspective. Philosophy East and West, Volume 64, Number 2,

April 2014, pp. 269-286

Bronk,K.C. A Grounded Theory of the Development of Noble Youth Purpose Journal of Adolescent Research27(1), 78–109. doi:10.1177/0743558411412958

Character education in UK schools. Research Report University of Birmingham 2015

Comte-Sponville, A. (2001). A small treatise on the great virtues (C. Temerson, Trans.). New York: Metropolitan Books

Curry, Oliver, Lee Rowland Sally Zlotowitz John McAlaney Harvey Whitehouse. Happy to Help? A systematic review and meta-analysis of the effects of performing acts of kindness on the well-being of the actor. *Open Science Framework*, 2016

Davidson, M., Lickona, T. and Khmelkov, V. (2008) 'Smart and Good Schools: A New

Paradigm for High School Character Education', in: Nucci, L. and Narvaez, D. (Eds.),

Handbook of Moral and Character Education, New York: Routledge

Duckworth,A. Peterson, C. Matthews. M D. Kelley D. R. Grit: Perseverance and Passion for Long-Term Goals July 2007 Journal of Personality and Social Psychology 92(6):1087-101

Emmons, R. A., & McCullough, M. E. (2003). Counting blessings versus burdens: An experimental investigation of gratitude and subjective well-being in daily life. Journal of Personality and Social Psychology,84, 377-389.

Fitzgerald, P. (1998). Gratitude and justice. Ethics, 109, 119–153.

Froh, J. J., Yurkewicz, C., & Kashdan, T. B. (2009). Gratitude and subjective well-being in early adolescence: Examining gender differences. Journal of Adolescence 32 633-650

Han, H. Purpose as a Moral Virtue for Flourishing. Journal of Moral Education

Georg Hegel. Philosophy of Right, I–II: Abstract Right and Morality

Goodman, M. L. Dickerson, A. S. Ness, R.B. Creativity in the Sciences: A Workbook Companion To Innovation Generation. Oxford University Press, U.S.A.; 1 edition (11 Jan. 2013)

Immanuel Kant. Critique of Practical Reason

Jubilee Centre for Character and Virtues (2013b) *A Framework for Character Education in Schools*, Birmingham: Jubilee Centre for Character and Virtues, University of Birmingham

John Locke. The Two Treatises of Government (1690),

Fen Xu, Xuehua Bao, Genyue Fu, Victoria Talwar, and Kang Lee Lying and Truth-Telling in Children: From Concept to Action Child Dev. 2010 Mar-Apr; 81(2): 581–596.

Held V. The Ethics of Care: Personal, Political, and Global. Oxford University Press 2006

Jackson, Jennifer. Truth, Tust and Medicine 2001 Routledge London

Barbara Misztal, Trust in Modern Societies: The Search for the Bases of Social Order, Polity Press, ISBN 0-7456-1634-8

Mccullough ME[1], Emmons RA, Tsang JA. The grateful disposition: a conceptual and empirical topography. Journal of Personality and Social Psychology. 2002 Jan;82(1):112-27.

Michael Michalko, Cracking Creativity Secrets of Creative Genius: The Secrets of Creative Genius for Business and Beyond. Ten Speed Press; New edition (26 Jun. 2001)

Blaise Pascal. The Provincial Letters

Pianalto, Matthew. On Patience: Reclaiming a Foundational Virtue. Lexington Books (1 Aug. 2017)

Friedrich Nietzsche, Twilight of the Idols

Reed, L. Jeremiah, J. Student Grit as an Important Ingredient for Academic and Personal Success. Page 252 Developments in Business Simulation and Experiential Learning, Volume 44, 201

Rotter, J.B. (1971).Generalized expectancies for interpersonal trust.American Psychologist, 26, 443 452

Shah, H., & Marks, N. (2004). A well-being manifesto for a flourishing society, London: The New Economics Foundation

Peterson, C. Seligman, M. Character Strengths and Virtues: A Handbook and Classification OUP USA (22 April 2004)

Promoting Grit, Tenacity, and Perseverance: *Critical Factors for Success in the 21st Century*. U.S. Department of Education. Office of Educational Technology. Prepared by: Nicole Shechtman. Angela H. DeBarger. Carolyn Dornsife. Soren Rosier. Louise Yarnall. Center for Technology in Learning. SRI international. Feb 1st 2013

Royce, J. 'The Philosophy of Loyalty', Macmillan 1908.

Alex Shaw, Vivian Li, Kristina R. Olson Children Apply Principles of Physical Ownership to Ideas. Cognitive Science 36 (2012) 1383–1403

Vigani, D. *"Is Patience a Virtue?" Journal of Value Inquiry, 2017, 51(2): 327–340.*

Walton, D. Courage: A Philosophical Investigation. University of California Press 1992

Wood, A. M., et al., Gratitude and well-being: A review and theoretical integration, Clinical Psychology Review (2010)

Walker,K.F.R,. Faculty Loyalty in High Priority Elementary Schools https://getd.libs.uga.edu/pdfs/walker_kay_r_200308_edd.pdf , Accessed April 2018

Xiao Pan Ding,[1] Danielle S. Omrin,[2] Angela D. Evans,[3] Genyue Fu,[1] Guopeng Chen,[4] and Kang Lee[2,5] Elementary School Children's Cheating Behavior and its Cognitive Correlates. J Exp Child Psychol. 2014 May; 121: 85–95.

Yearley, L. H. (1990). Mencius and Aquinas: Theories of virtue and conceptions of courage.Albany: State University of New York Press

www.kidscanpress.com/sites/default/files/products/assets/MostMagnificentThingThe_2177_t eaching_2.pdf   Accessed March 11th 2018

www.Inspiremykids.com   Acessed 27th February 2018

www.lifelessons4u.wordpress.com/tag/benefits-of-patience/

www.magnificentkids.com.au/i-am-magnificent-.html   Accessed 12th April 2018

www.//virtuefirst.org/virtues/loyalty/   Accessed March 8th 2018

https://talkingtreebooks.com/definition/what-is-honesty.html Accessed 13 February 2018

www.hvparent.com/early-friendships-profoundly-affects-childs-development   Accessed 22nd February 2018

www.handsonscotland.co.uk/flourishing_and_wellbeing_in_children_and_young_people/sen se_of_purpose/sense_of_purpose.html   Accessed March 19th 2018

www.simplyphilosophy.org/study/ownership-as-a-moral-right/   Accessed April 5th 2018

www.lifelessons4u.wordpress.com/tag/benefits-of-patience/

www.talkingtreebooks.com/definition/what-is-perseverance
Accessed March 11th 2018

www.outre-monde.com/2015/01/03/the-lost-virtue-of-patience/   Accessed April 8th 2018

www.wisdomtimes.com/blog/importance-of-patience-in-life/   Accessed April 10th 2018

www.huffingtonpost.com/dr-hyder-zahed/patience-is-a-virtue-worth-developing   Accessed
April 10th 2018

www.mcgill.ca/connectionslab/files/connectionslab/peer_relationships_1.pdf   Accessed
April 13th 2018

www.cyh.com/HealthTopics/HealthTopicDetailsKids.aspx?p=335&id=1636&np=286
Accessed April 17th 2018

www.leadershipthoughts.com/build-team-loyalty-commitment-trust
Accessed April 19th 2018

https://health.usnews.com/wellness/for-parents/articles/2018-02-05/talking-to-kids-about-the-tricky-trait-of-loyalty   Accessed April 22nd 2018

www.psychologytoday.com/us/blog/growing-friendships   Accessed April 22nd 2018

www.bbc.co.uk/ethics/introduction/intro_1.shtml   Accessed April 29th 2018

www.scribd.com/doc/6877665/honesty-for-kids   Accessed May 1st 2018

www.trueaimeducation.com/values-for-children-teach-honesty   Accessed May 1st 2018

https://en.wikipedia.org/wiki/Trust_(emotion)#cite_note-BarbaraMisztal-32
Accessed May 1st 2018

https://plato.stanford.edu/entries/trust/   Accessed May 1st 2018

http://www.gettysburgtimes.com/app/nie/trustworthiness.pdf   Accessed May 2018

http://4h.missouri.edu/showmecharacter/trustcc#gsc.tab=0   Accessed May 3rd 2018

http://www.cocha-banner.org/issues/2016/february/the-importance-of-trust/
Accessed May 4th 2018

https://creatingcurriculum.wordpress.com/2014/06/14/the-ups-and-downs-of-being-a-gifted-child/   Accessed May 31st 2018